YOUR KNOWLEDGE HAS VALUE

- We will publish your bachelor's and
  master's thesis, essays and papers

- Your own eBook and book -
  sold worldwide in all relevant shops

- Earn money with each sale

Upload your text at www.GRIN.com
and publish for free

Marco Schönberger

The Demonic Nature of Evil in Shakespeare's Plays

An Approach

GRIN Verlag

Bibliografische Information der Deutschen Nationalbibliothek:

Die Deutsche Bibliothek verzeichnet diese Publikation in der Deutschen National-bibliografie; detaillierte bibliografische Daten sind im Internet über http://dnb.d-nb.de/ abrufbar.

Imprint:

Copyright © 2011 GRIN Verlag GmbH
Druck und Bindung: Books on Demand GmbH, Norderstedt Germany
ISBN: 978-3-656-55312-0

This book at GRIN:

http://www.grin.com/en/e-book/265676/the-demonic-nature-of-evil-in-shakespeare-s-plays

GRIN - Your knowledge has value

Der GRIN Verlag publiziert seit 1998 wissenschaftliche Arbeiten von Studenten, Hochschullehrern und anderen Akademikern als eBook und gedrucktes Buch. Die Verlagswebsite www.grin.com ist die ideale Plattform zur Veröffentlichung von Hausarbeiten, Abschlussarbeiten, wissenschaftlichen Aufsätzen, Dissertationen und Fachbüchern.

Visit us on the internet:

http://www.grin.com/

http://www.facebook.com/grincom

http://www.twitter.com/grin_com

The Demonic Nature
of Evil
in Shakespeare's Plays

An Approach

by Marco Schönberger

Table of Contents

Evil – a Word so Difficult to Define

Evil, what is the definition of evil?

There are certain things which everyone immediately associates with the term of 'evil' and for sure some of them will come to everyone's mind as soon as we hear the word 'evil'. We think of persons like Adolf Hitler, Josef Stalin or Osama Bin Laden and deeds like killing, stealing or destroying other persons' property.

But although there are certain patterns of evil which seem plausible to any reasonable person in this world, we cannot apply them to each and any of us, as everyone has got his/her own perception of what is evil and what is not. Even if the majority of mankind on the first hand would say it is wrong to kill a person, there still might be some cases in which we think differently. It might well be possible to say killing a person is right if the concerned person wishes so for any reasons he/she believes to be enough to be longing for death (health reasons, family problems, …), but is not able to end his/her life for him-/herself for whatever reason (unable to move, …). Another thing which in some persons' opinion justifies killing a person is death penalty. They say a person who has killed someone else deserves death. Yet another thing which must be mentioned is arbitrary law. There are persons who say acting in revenge exculpates certain deeds, even killing.

So, if we cannot define the word 'evil' by any persons or actions which are to be considered as evil, is there any other possibility of reaching a conclusion about this word so difficult to determine? We could try and have a closer look on the religious view of the topic, where being evil means breaking God-given rules.

If we just take the Catholic religion as an example we will see that – considering the Ten Commandments – the God-given rules also condemn murder and robbery, which partly fits the image of evil which many people have. We could say that the deeds to be condemned by mankind (i.e. doing something illegal) are a summary of the things which every single of us considers as evil. It therefore is evil to break the law. But where does this law come from? As we have already seen, it is kind of convention containing the majority's opinion about what is evil and what is not, which in its term originally comes from moral conventions (such as God-given rules like the Ten Commandments).

As a conclusion we might say evil is what God forbids, but is this really a satisfying result? At this point we might refer to one of the greatest and best-known playwrights ever, who has dealt a lot with the topic of evil in every aspect, William Shakespeare.

This might lead us to a better understanding of the term 'evil' in all its facets, or at least the perception of evil which people had in Shakespeare's times.

1 Shakespeare's Source of Inspiration

In order to get an idea what Shakespeare's opinion about evil was, me must have many things in mind, and it certainly is not an easy task to find out what his idea of malignity was, as we do not know much about Shakespeare himself, but have to draw a conclusion about his idea of evil from the content of his plays.

Having a look at the plays in order to distinguish what Shakespeare thought of evil, in turn we have a problem. Shakespeare was not a playwright, whose own ideas can be clearly seen in his plays, as he also incorporated certain things just in order to characterize the persons in his plays and to push the plot on.

So, how can we distinguish which parts of his plays are his own body of thought and which are pure fiction?

This question is quite difficult to answer, and in order to find an appropriate response to it, it is necessary to have a look at Shakespeare's vita. Doing so, we will learn that Shakespeare was a strictly religious, more precisely Protestant, man, which can be seen in many things such as his last will.[1] All the allusions to the Bible or even quotes from it to be found in his plays permit the conclusion that Shakespeare had a vast knowledge of the Bible. But this broad acquaintance with the Holy Book not only shows Shakespeare's Christianity, but also his Protestantism, as the Catholic Church in those days combated the circulation of the Bible among laymen.[2]

His religion obviously has influenced the way in which Shakespeare wrote and as we just mentioned there are many allusions to the Bible, although Shakespeare's plays certainly are not purely religious, just as they do not exclusively reflect his ideas.

Even if we do not have any more helpful information about Shakespeare himself for our task to find out what Shakespeare's idea of evil was, there is one more hint for Shakespeare's own ideas to be found: If Shakespeare repeatedly used certain patterns of evil and always characterized them as being bad deeds, it shows a tendency of what Shakespeare wanted to seem evil and what not.

---

1 Cf. Eckhardt, section 55
2 Cf. Eckhardt, sections 9f

2 Appearance of Evil in Shakespeare's Plays

Having in mind the findings from chapter 1, we now might try to analyse Shakespeare's evil characters and certain images of evil which repeatedly appear in the plays.

In order to do so, I would like to pick out some of Shakespeare's plays and characters who seem to be evil and classify them by the sort of bad deed committed, in order to be able to analyse them one after another to finally reach a conclusion about recurring patterns – and Shakespeare's own idea – of evil.

2.1 Incest

> "*Locutusque est Dominus ad Mosen dicens* [...].
> *facietis iudicia mea et praecepta servabitis et ambulabitis in eis.* [...]
> **omnis homo ad proximam sanguinis sui non accedet ut revelet turpitudinem eius**
> *ego Dominus Deus vester.*"[3]
>
> (Accentuation by writer)

> "*And the LORD spake* [*sic*] *unto Moses, saying,*
> *Ye shall do my judgments* [*sic*]*, and keep mine ordinances, to walk therein* [...]
> **None of you shall approach to any that is near of kin to him, to uncover their nakedness.**
> *I am the Lord.*"[4]
>
> (Accentuation by writer)

By saying these words, God prohibited Moses and his entire people to have sex with any relatives, so to say, to inbreed.

As we know that Shakespeare was a very religious man himself, we can assume he disagreed with incestuous relationships, which can also be proved by having a look at two of his plays where incest plays a rather big role.

---

3 Fischer, Biblia Sacra: Leviticus 18: 1, 4, 6
4 Project Gutenberg, King James Bible: Leviticus 18: 1, 4, 6

2.1.1 "Hamlet": Claudius and Gertrude

"[…] father and mother is man and wife;
man and wife is one flesh […]."[5]

This is a quote from one of the greatest and best-known Shakespearean plays, "Hamlet, Prince of Denmark".

This play deals with the topic of the young Prince of Denmark, whose father Old Hamlet has just passed away. After Old Hamlet's death, his brother Claudius almost immediately marries Gertrude, Old Hamlet's widow, supposedly to keep the Danish Empire strong against attacks from foreign countries, particularly the Norwegian forces under Fortinbras. However, during the play, Young Hamlet discovers that his father did not die a natural death, but has been killed scrupulously by Claudius, who wanted to seize power in the empire. Later on Young Hamlet decides to take revenge on his father's murderer, but has to face many more displeasures until he succeeds.

Roughly knowing the plot of the play, at first glance, one would not say this is a play about incest, and it certainly is true that it was not Shakespeare's intention to write a play about incest, but there are some scenes in which incest appears and is strongly criticised within the play.

The very quote I elected for introducing this play deals with incest, which anyway cannot be recognized easily without going deeper into the topic. Even if nowadays no one would consider it as incest, in fact the Bible, which is to say God, prohibits a relationship between a man and his brother's wife:

"Thou shalt not uncover the nakedness of thy brother's wife: it is thy brother's nakedness."[6]

Consequentially, in Shakespeare's time it must have been considered as incestuous and a bad deed to marry one's brother-/sister-in-law, as people in those days were quite religious, just as Shakespeare himself.

Aforementioned quote refers to that very topic. It originates from a dialogue between Hamlet and Claudius and what Hamlet wants to express by saying these words to Claudius is that, by marrying Gertrude, he has sort of married his sister, as Gertrude was his brother's wife and "[…] *man and wife is one flesh* […]".[7]

---

5 Markus, Hamlet: Act IV Scene 3, l. 58f
6 Project Gutenberg, King James Bible: Leviticus 18: 16
7 Markus, Hamlet: Act IV Scene 3, l. 59

This permits the reverse conclusion that Gertrude also inbreeds by marrying her dead husband's – which is to say her own – brother. To confirm this, I would like to show that Gertrude also is accused of being incestuous, by quoting from the play again, this time from an extract of one of Hamlet's monologues, where he accuses his mother of inbreeding by marrying Claudius, at that even being overhasty, doing so only one month after her husband's death:

> "[…] *why she, even she –*
> *[…] a beast that wants discourse of reason*[8]
> *would have mourn'd longer – married with my*
> *uncle,*
> *My father's brother.*
> *[…]*
> *O most wicked speed, to post*
> *with such dexterity to incestuous sheets!*"[9]

There are many other passages within the play which could be mentioned concerning incest, but this would lead too far. I think it is clearly visible that Shakespeare completely disagreed with incestuous relationships, as the hero of the play, Hamlet, continuously condemns his mother's and uncle's behaviour.

Yet another fact which fortifies this theory is that both Claudius and Gertrude have to die at the end of the play, which is the destiny of all of Shakespeare's evil characters, as we will see again later on. This also can be linked to the Bible, where it is said that "[…] *the wages of sin is death* […]"[10], which in turn can be linked to Shakespeare's religious belief. We can assume that Shakespeare knew this part of the Bible or at least the idea of punishment by death, which he applies to all the sinners in his works.

I would like to close the topic of incest in "Hamlet" by giving a last quote, the quote which closures the theme of incest in the play, namely the words Hamlet says to Claudius when killing him, after Gertrude has already died:

> "*Here, thou incestuous, murd'rous, damned Dane,*
> *Drink of this potion.* […]
> *Follow my mother.*"[11]

---

8 "wants discourse of reason" ≙ "lacks the capacity of rational thought" (Markus, Hamlet: p. 34)
9 Markus, Hamlet: Act I Scene 2, l. 151 – 159
10 Project Gutenberg, King James Bible: Romans 6: 23
11 Markus, Hamlet: Act V Scene 2, l. 345ff

2.1.2 "Pericles": *Antiochus and His Daughter*

To fortify the thesis that Shakespeare disagreed with incestuous relationships, I would like to present another Shakespearean play which tells the story of a young woman who was …

> *"So buxom, blithe and full of face,*
> *as heaven had lent her all his grace;*
> *With whom the father liking took,*
> *and **her to incest did provoke**:"*[12]
>
> (Accentuation by writer)

This quote is taken from one of the least known Shakespearean plays, "Pericles, Prince of Tyre"

The play partly is about a beautiful young lady, whose father Antiochus seduces her to incest after her mother has died. To ensure that he can keep his daughter for himself, he asks all her lovers a riddle, which is as follows:

> *"I am no viper, yet I feed*
> *On mother's flesh which did me breed.*
> *I sought a husband, in which labour*
> *I found that kindness in a father.*
> *He's father, son and husband mild;*
> *I mother, wife, and yet his child.*
> *How they may be, and yet in two,*
> *As you will live resolve it you."*[13]

It is essential to solve it in order to be allowed to marry Antiochus' daughter. If a candidate does not know the riddle's answer, he will be condemned to death immediately.

Just like many other young men before him, who have lost their lives for the inability to solve the riddle, Pericles – the hero of the play – also asks Antiochus for his beautiful daughter's hand. When it comes to solve above-quoted riddle, Antiochus tells Pericles to "[…] *expound now*[14] *or receive [his] sentence*[15]."[16], whereon Pericles responds that – in his believe – "*few love to hear the sins they love to act.*"[17] This means Pericles knows the riddle's answer, as the riddle refers to the incestuous relationship between Antiochus and his daughter, which is the sin Antiochus acts and which he wants to hear about by asking for the riddle's answer.

The king now condemns Pericles to death for not solving the riddle, which according to Antiochus is right as Pericles has not pronounced the answer itself, but only an allusion to it.

---

12 Pelli-Ehrensperger, Pericles: Act I Prologue, l. 23 - 26
13 Pelli-Ehrensperger, Pericles: Act I Scene 1, l. 65 - 72
14 i.e. say the answer to the riddle
15 i.e. the death sentence
16 Pelli-Ehrensperger, Pericles: Act I Scene 1, l. 91
17 Pelli-Ehrensperger, Pericles: Act I Scene 1, l. 93

As we can see, the relationship between Antiochus and his daughter is something completely wrong to do, which probably also was what Shakespeare wanted to express. Antiochus not only inbreeds, but he also murders in order to continue the relationship with his daughter. This behaviour causes the reader to completely disprize Antiochus, which supposedly was Shakespeare's intention, which can be concluded from the fact Shakespeare was a great playwright and knew how to affect the audience of his plays.

Again, the topic of incest appears recurrently during the whole play, until the two sinners Antiochus and his daughter die, which is another strong hint that Shakespeare wanted incest to seem quite a bad thing to do, as he never adds any mitigating circumstances.

As I have already said, Shakespeare's evil characters always come to a miserable end, which again can be seen in this play. In the 4th scene of the second act Helicanus tells Escanes[18] that *"Antiochus from incest [lives] not free [...]"*[19], whereupon *"[...] the most high [sic] gods [...]"*[20] can no longer *"[...] withhold the vengeance that they [have] in store, Due to this heinous capital offense"*[21]. For the sin Antiochus and his daughter act they are consequentially punished by heaven when a *"[...] fire from heaven [comes] and [shrivels] up their bodies [...]"*[22]

The fire from heaven apparently – as Helicanus also mentions – is to be seen as a represen-tation of the Gods, who condemn Antiochus and his daughter for inbreeding. Shakespeare in this play obviously refers to more than one God, as the play is set in ancient Greece. Even if so, we might again link this scene to Shakespeare's Christianity, leaving apart the fact that more than one God appears.[23] Heavenly vengeance is a motive which is often used in Christian belief as well, and incest – as we could already see – is a really bad sin in accordance with the Bible.

Shakespeare also opens and closures this play with exactly the same theme: incest. This is another indication that Shakespeare really had the intention to convince the audience of the immorality of incest. In the prologue of the first scene he lets Gower tell us about the relationship between Antiochus and his daughter and in the epilogue again Gower picks up this motive by telling the audience that *"[in] Antiochus and his daughter [they] have heard of monstrous lust the due and just reward"*[24]

---

18 Helicanus and Escanes: two lords of Tyre
19 Pelli-Ehrensperger, Pericles: Act II Scene 4, l. 2
20 Pelli-Ehrensperger, Pericles: Act II Scene 4, l. 3
21 Pelli-Ehrensperger, Pericles: Act II Scene 4, l. 4f
22 Pelli-Ehrensperger, Pericles: Act II Scene 4, l. 9f
23 See chapter 1: Usage of certain things just for the plot's development
24 Pelli-Ehrensperger, Pericles: Act V Epilogue, l. 1f

2.1.3 Summary

Summarizing the findings about incest from "Hamlet" and "Pericles", we can see the following concordances:

- In both plays incest is not only mentioned once, but the motive develops and appears recurrently during the entire play.

- All of the persons inbreeding have to die in the end. And both times we could say it is a heavenly sentence, whereat in "Hamlet" Hamlet himself is the medium of vengeance and in "Pericles" it is the fire from the skies.

- Shakespeare never adds any alleviating factors which would defend the relationships mentioned above.

Adding the knowledge about Shakespeare's Christianity and the malignity of incest according to the Bible, we must say incest was quite an important thing for Shakespeare, which must not be done by any means.

Even if nowadays merely few people would say a relationship with one's brother-/sister-in-law is incestuous, Shakespeare's opinion about incest still quite fits the modern credos: It is something to be misprized by everyone and to be judged by the powers that be.

2.2 Pessimism

> *"an nescitis quoniam membra vestra templum est Spiritus Sancti qui in vobis est*
> *quem habetis a Deo et non estis vestri*
> *empti enim estis pretio magno **glorificate et portate Deum in corpore vestro.**"*[25]
>
> (Accentuation by writer)

> *"What? Know ye not that your body is the temple of the Holy Ghost which is in you,*
> *which ye have of God and ye are not your own?*
> *For ye are bought with a price: **therefore glorify God in your body** […].*"[26]
>
> (Accentuation by writer)

This quote from the Bible deals with the topic of pessimism insofar as it tells us to honour God with our bodies, i.e. to serve God and to fulfil a certain task for him. It tells us our bodies are not our own property, but property of the Lord, which means that we are not allowed in any way to murder or to commit suicide, as it is not subject to our, but only to God's might to end our lives.

---

25 Fischer, Biblia Sacra: Ad Corinthios I 6: 19f
26 Project Gutenberg, King James Bible: 1st Corinthians 6: 19f

A Shakespearean play which deals with pessimism and suicidal thoughts is "Hamlet, Prince of Denmark" and next I would like to have a closer look on the appearance of pessimism in this play.

2.2.1 "Hamlet": The Prince Himself

> "To be, or not to be - that is the question;
> Whether 'tis nobler in the mind to suffer
> The slings and arrows of outrageous fortune,
> Or to take arms against a sea of troubles,
> And by opposing end them? *To die, to sleep* –
> No more; and by a sleep to say we end
> The heart-ache and the thousand natural shocks
> That flesh is heir to. 'Tis *a consummation*
> *Devoutly to be wish'd. To die, to sleep.*"[27]
>
> (Accentuation by writer)

This is another quote from Shakespeare's "Hamlet, Prince of Denmark" and certainly will not be the last, as this play contains many patterns of evil. The quote above is one of the most cited passages from all the Shakespearean plays and there are lots of controversies about its interpretation, although to me it is quite clear that this is where Hamlet's pessimism and his suicidal thoughts show up. He deliberates about whether he should continue suffering his fortune inwardly or do something about it by fighting it. Then his suicidal thoughts come up again and he thinks of the eternal sleep that would liberate him from all the displeasures life provides him with.

According to the Bible, God wants us to serve his will and fulfil the mission he has given us for our life, which is exactly what Hamlet doubts. He does not want to carry on with his life, which has bestowed much turbulence for him to transcend.

Particular pessimism can be seen in many passages during the entire play, which means we have to do with a theme that develops during the whole play again, which is a strong indication that Shakespeare wanted it to seem important. I would like to give only one more example where Hamlet's suicidal thoughts can be seen:

> "O, that this too solid flesh would melt,
> Thaw, and resolve itself into a dew!
> Or that the Everlasting had not fix'd
> His canon 'gainst self-slaughter! O God! God!"[28]

---

27 Markus, Hamlet: Act III Scene 1, l. 63 - 71
28 Markus, Hamlet: Act I Scene 2, l. 131 - 134

This shows that Hamlet no doubt is aware that suicide would be a sin, as he mentions the God-given canon against it. Even if so, he still longs for death, as he says he pities the fact that said biblical law[29] exists.

Even if he regrets his thoughts of killing himself for the knowledge he is a sinner hence, Hamlet never stops longing for death, which means he never stops being a sinner. Anyway, God – according to the Bible – is satisfied with the sinners' repentance to forgive them.

2.2.2 Summary

Again comparing all the findings about Hamlet's pessimism, we will find the following points which support the idea Hamlet for Shakespeare was evil:

- Pessimism and suicidal thoughts are something completely wrong according to Christian belief, they even can be seen as blasphemy.
- The theme again develops during the entire play, which leads to the conclusion Shakespeare assumed it to be important.
- Hamlet has to die, which could be seen as heavenly punishment.

Even if so, there can also be found arguments against aforementioned thesis:

- Hamlet regrets his actions, which means God should forgive him.
- Hamlet dies a heroic death, which argues against the thesis it is heavenly justice.

Overall, we could say there are plausible arguments both for and against our thesis, which means we cannot draw a conclusion with the means we have. Nevertheless, we might assume that Hamlet's pessimism rather serves to push on the plot than to demonstrate Shakespeare's own opinion about the theme.

---

29 See chapter 2.2: Our bodies are property of God

2.3 *Murder*

> "*ego sum Dominus Deus tuus qui eduxi te*
> *de terra Aegypti de domo servitutis.*
> [...]
> **Non occides.**"[30]

> (Accentuation by writer)

> "*I am the LORD thy God, which have* [sic] *brought thee*
> *out of the land of Egypt, out of the house of bondage.*
> [...]
> **Thou shalt not kill.**"[31]

> (Accentuation by writer)

This quote is taken from the Ten Commandments, which – according to the Bible – Moses received directly from God at the holy mountain Sinai. As can be seen, God explicitly prohibits the violent finalization of our brothers' and sisters' lives.

When trying to analyse Shakespeare's plays concerning murder, we will see that there are many different persons who kill their fellow men, which makes the work quite complicated. Anyway, murder definitely is the most important pattern of evil used by Shakespeare and thus must not be left out. Anyhow, not all the killings that appear in Shakespeare's plays can be considered as evil actions, subject to their motivations and other circumstances.

In order to find out the murders to be considered as evil in Shakespeare's plays, I would like to have a closer look at "Hamlet" again, before analysing "Macbeth" concerning the crime of killing.

2.3.1 "Hamlet": Claudius

> "CLAUDIUS:
> *'O, my offence is rank, it smells to heaven;*
> *It hath the primal eldest curse upon't –*
> *A brother's murder!'*"[32]

As we already know[33], Claudius murders Old Hamlet in order to marry Gertrude and to seize power in the empire, which must be seen as murder by any means, be it a modern or an ancient definition of murder. The modern definition of murder is the killing of another person with bad intentions, which certainly applies to Claudius, as he only puts his brother to death for his own benefit.

---

30 Fischer, Biblia Sacra: Exodus 20: 2;13
31 Project Gutenberg, King James Bible: Exodus 20: 2;13
32 Markus, Hamlet: Act III Scene 3, l. 39ff
33 See chapter 2.1.1: Incest between Claudius and Gertrude

The whole play almost exclusively deals with this murder so foul it really causes scornful-
ness. This is one hint Shakespeare wanted this murder to seem evil, as it directs the whole
plot of the play.

The Bible condemns murder, which can be taken from the Ten Commandments. Here the
knowledge about Shakespeare's religion comes in handy, as we can say Shakespeare must
have been against killing all the same.

In this case, there even can be found two aggravating factors which make Claudius' deed
even worse:

- Claudius kills a king!

  Nowadays, we would say there is no difference if you murder a politician or a
  beggar; everyone is equal under the law. But in Shakespeare's time people used to
  think that their sovereigns were the direct representatives of God, which means
  killing a king meant to question and undercut the Lord's will, which in turn signi-
  fied to blaspheme. This derives from the following quote:

  > "Let every soul be subject unto the higher powers. For there is no power but of God: the
  > powers that be are ordained of God. Whosoever therefore resisteth the power, resisteth the
  > ordinance of God: and they that resist shall receive to themselves damnation"[34]

- Claudius never feels sorry for his deed, which would be essential for God to forgive
  him, as we could already see before.[35] We might therefore say Claudius has done
  something terrible, namely murdered and blasphemed, and does not even feel sorry
  about it, which means he should be condemned by God forever.

As can be seen, in the end Claudius is executed by Hamlet, which means he is punished by
God for his sins[36], whereat Hamlet is the instrument of God's will.

This consequentially – together with other factors – means Hamlet is not to be seen as evil
for the killings he does, as he kills Polonius and Laertes unintentionally and afterwards
regrets having done so, and murders Claudius for vengeance[37] and as part of God-given
justice. Normally, Hamlet's killings would have been dealt with in a separate chapter, but
due to the restricted space I will have to neglect it. Besides, the conclusion that Hamlet is
not to be condemned for his murders would have been reached all the same, with the same
arguments, but more detailed.

---

34 Project Gutenberg, King James Bible: Romans 13: 1f
35 See chapter 2.2.1: Dispensation of sins
36 See chapter 2.1.1: Death as heavenly justice
37 In Shakespeare's time arbitrary law was not seen as a bad thing to do. Also see "eye for eye, tooth for
   tooth [...]" (Project Gutenberg, King James Bible: Exodus 21: 24)

2.3.2 "Macbeth": Macbeth and His Lady

"I go, and it is done. The bell invites me.
Hear it not, Duncan, for it is a knell
That summons thee to heaven or to hell."[38]

This quote, taken from one of the best-known and most-interpreted Shakespearean plays, "Macbeth", is said by Duncan's killer right before doing his dirty deed.

Macbeth is a military leader under king Duncan of Scotland, who receives a promotion after winning an important fight and killing a traitor. Before even being told about the promotion by official sources, three witches prophecy it to him. The three witches also tell him he soon will be king himself, which Macbeth immediately tells his wife. Lady Macbeth instantaneously thinks of killing Duncan, as she does not believe that her husband will become king legally. She tries to convince her husband, who does not agree until Duncan elects his son and not Macbeth as heir to the throne.[39] As the king is planning to visit Macbeth's castle, Macbeth and his wife start to make preparations to kill Duncan, which in the end also is done by them, more exactly by Macbeth himself.

On the first hand only Lady Macbeth seems to be evil, as Macbeth himself does not show big interest in the throne if this means killing the beloved king. Lady Macbeth is the one who plans and prepares everything for the murder, which means she must be seen as evil in certain way. She plans a bad deed, which finally is also done. What safes Lady Macbeth is that the longer the deed has passed the more she regrets it. She goes mental and finally commits suicide for the guilt she feels and the good inside her, which she tries to hide. Anyhow, at the end she feels truly bad about what her husband and she have done. This means God ought to forgive her[40], even if he punishes her.[41]

The really malicious character in this play is Macbeth himself. Even if at the beginning he does not like the idea of killing, he does not regret his deed afterwards, as he has achieved lots of benefits by killing Duncan. In order to be able to keep these benefits, he even continues killing – even though only on charge – more and more persons who endanger his power. He does not even shy away from having innocent children killed, completely possessed by his hunger for power.

---

38 Pulverness, Macbeth: Act II Scene 1, l. 62ff
39 In Scotland the royal family's children not automatically were heir to the throne, but someone was elected.
   Until that moment Macbeth still had a chance to become king without any complot.
40 See chapter 2.2.1: Dispensation of sins
41 Mental disease and afterwards death as a punishment by God

Yet, he has to pay for his cruel deeds, as in the end he is killed by the sword of one of Duncan's avengers, which again could be seen as heavenly justice.

Again, the same aggravating factors as could be seen with Claudius appear here:

- Killing a king:

    As we have already seen above, killing a king for Shakespeare must have been something completely wrong to do as it incorporated worst blasphemy in some way for the reasons explained above.

- Macbeth does not show any remorse for what he has done, as he has become a completely materialistic person, who does not care any longer about honour or justice. Lady Macbeth regrets her deeds and therefore shall not be seen as evil as Macbeth himself.

2.3.3 Summary

Summarizing the achievements from chapters *2.3.1* and *2.3.2*, we can see that not every person who murders in Shakespeare's plays is to be considered as an evil person. Whether a killer can be seen as evil or not depends on some factors and as a conclusion to this topic we might bring them all as follows:

A murderer for Shakespeare is evil, if ...

- ... he/she does not regret his/her deed, which means he/she is satisfied with what he/she has done – either for avarice or for unscrupulousness.

- ... he or she does not act in vengeance. Revenge in certain cases exculpates murder, e.g. if the murdered person has killed a close and beloved relative with malice intentions.

One thing that must be seen as absolutely evil is regicide. To kill a king not only means murdering, but also blaspheming, which having in mind the prevailing circumstances must have been seen as something completely disrespectable both by Shakespeare's contemporaries as by himself.[42]

---

42 See chapter 2.3.1: King as representative of God

3 Conclusion

In order to summarize the findings from the entire work, first of all I would like to repeat that all the motives of evil dealt with in this work can be seen as evil. The only one that may have left doubts is pessimism but we have to say that pessimism in a certain way of course can be seen as evil, even if Hamlet cannot be considered a bad person for being pessimistic.[43]

Overall, all the images of evil used by Shakespeare could be summarized with one word: Blasphemy.

Incest can be seen as blasphemous as it dishonours the human beings, who are a counterpart of God, which means it would dishonour God himself in some way. Pessimism is to be seen as blasphemy insofar as God made us for a special assignment, which means being pessimistic and having suicidal thoughts stands for dishonouring God's will. And last but not least, murder – especially regicide – signifies destroying something God-given and not accepting the Lord's will again. Even if the killed person is not royal, he still has been set on earth by God.

Even if this is quite a dubious interpretation of the things, at least we can say that all of the Shakespearean characters who are evil commit a deed condemned by the church, which means the patterns of evil used by Shakespeare all derive from religion.

Another way of interpreting all the achievements made in the second chapter is that not one of the presented patterns of evil really represents Shakespeare's thoughts. As we have already seen in chapter 1, Shakespeare's plays sometimes do not say much about the playwright himself, but are used exclusively for the development of the plot. Maybe all the evil persons in Shakespeare's plays only are a means to an end, namely to catch the audience's attention.

But we must admit that the thesis about Shakespeare's disagreement with sins and affection towards the Christian belief – represented by the condemnation of all the sinners in the plays – seems much more plausible. Thus, we can say that a big part of Shakespeare's life-work reflects this great playwright's real life and reveals his likings and dislikes.

---

43 See chapter 2.2.2: Arguments against malignity of Hamlet's pessimism

Not even Shakespeare Knew more about It

As to give a résumé for the entire work, first of all I would like to mention that much more Shakespearean plays should have been dealt with in order to grab the complex question profoundly what the images of evil used by a great playwright like Shakespeare – who has written too many plays to list them all right here – were. Works like "Othello" or "King Lear" would have been nice to mention, and more patterns of evil could have been found.

Anyhow, I feel the most important aspects have been dealt with and we could learn something quite interesting about Shakespeare and his life by analysing his works:

Shakespeare's perception of good and evil is guided by his Christian belief.

If we remember our initial try to define evil, we found out that evil might be determined as a summary of certain moral conventions, which each and any of us has got from his parents, after it has been passed on for generations. And the moral conventions somehow also derive from the Bible, reaching back to the time when nearly everyone was Christian in Europe.

Could we therefore say Shakespeare did not know more about evil than we do? Do our findings mean there is an obvious link between religious rules and everyone's idea of evil? And, might we say certain God-like things such as the idea of evil have never been deposited?

Maybe. And maybe we all are steered by the Almighty without even knowing it!

Bibliography

In this chapter, the works cited in the text are listed:

[1]   Eckhardt, Eduard. 1940. *Shakespeare's Anschauungen über Religion und Sittlichkeit, Staat und Volk*. In: Keller, Wolfgang (Ed.). Schriften der deutschen Shakespeare-Gesellschaft Band IV. Weimar: Hermann Böhlaus Nachfolger.

[2]   Fischer, B.; Gribomont, I.; Sparks, H.; Thiele, W. (Eds.). 1923. *Biblia Sacra: Iuxta Vulgatam Versionem (3rd ed.)*. Stuttgart: Deutsche Bibelgesellschaft.

[3]   Markus, Julia; Jordan, Paul (Eds.). 2006. *Hamlet. William Shakespeare (15th ed.)*. Essex: Longman Group.

[4]   Pelli-Ehrensperger, Annabarbara (Ed.). 2005. *William Shakespeare. Pericles, Prince of Tyre. Pericles, Fürst von Tyrus*. Tübingen: Stauffenburg Verlag.

[5]   Project Gutenberg (Ed.). 1992. *King James Bible (Second Version, 10th Edition)*. Electronic book. Champaign: Project Gutenberg.

[6]   Pulverness, Alan; Schroeder-Thürauf, Susanne (Eds). 2008. *William Shakespeare. Macbeth*. Berlin: Cornelsen.

Advanced Bibliography

This chapter contains a list of the books, which have been inspected for the preparation of this work, but not been cited:

[1]   Bayley, Harold. 1906. *The Shakespeare Symphony. An Introduction to the Ethics of the Elizabethan Drama.* London: Chapman and Hall Ltd.

[2]   Knight, George Wilson. 1967. *Shakespeare and Religion. essays of forty years.* London: Routledge & Kegan Paul

[3]   Manning, Roger B. 1969. *Religion and Society in Elizabethan Sussex. A study of the enforcement of the religious settlement 1558 - 1603.* Bristol: Leicester University Press.

[4]   Sears, Lloyd C. 1974. *Shakespeare's Philosophy of Evil.* North Quincy: The Christopher Publishing House.

[5]   Spivack, Bernard. 1958. *Shakespeare and the Allegory of Evil. The History of a Metaphor in Relation to his Major Villains.* New York: Columbia University Press.